# Count to a
# MILLION

# 1,000,000

## by Jerry Pallotta
## Illustrated by Rob Bolster

### SCHOLASTIC INC.

New York   Toronto   London   Auckland   Sydney   Mexico City   New Delhi   Hong Kong   Buenos Aires

*A million thanks to Pat Young, Reba Wadsworth, Willie and Glenda Pentecost, Carolyn Brown, and Mary Ann Inderbitzen.*
—*Jerry Pallotta*
*This book is dedicated to Aunt Rose.*
—*Rob Bolster*

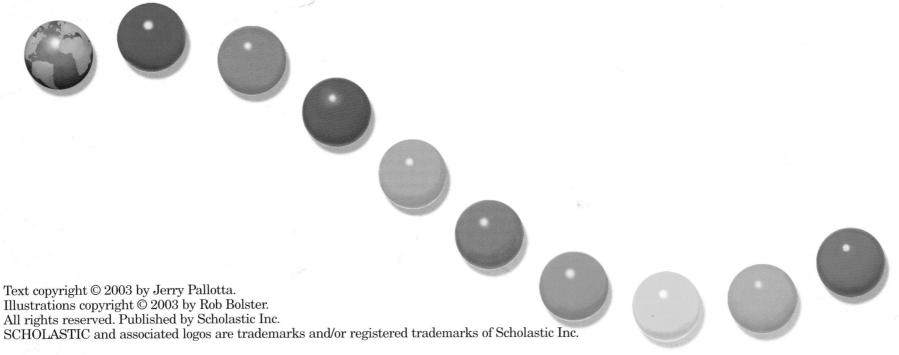

Library of Congress Cataloging-in-Publication Data available.

ISBN 0-439-38915-1

12 11 10 9 8 7 6 5 4 3                    3   4   5   6   7   8/0

Printed in the U.S.A.
First printing, January 2003

# 1
# ONE

If you can count to ten, you can count to one million.
Welcome to the decimal system.

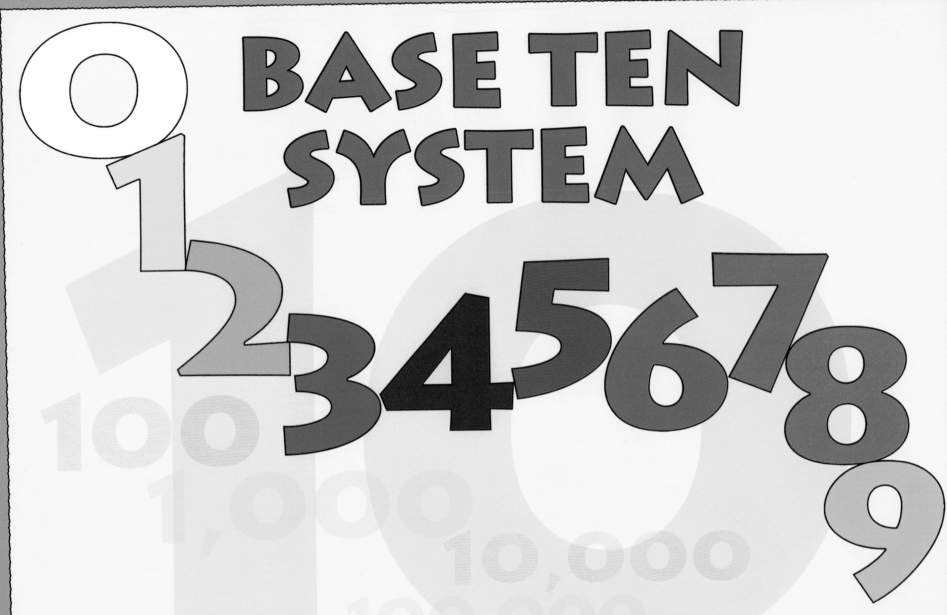

# BASE TEN SYSTEM

You can count to one million using just ten numerals.
They are: 0, 1, 2, 3, 4, 5, 6, 7, 8, 9.
This number system is called the
DECIMAL SYSTEM, or the BASE TEN SYSTEM.
Numbers using one numeral are called single-digit numbers.

Look at these grains of sand. They have been magnified so you can see them easily. Count to ten. One, two, three, four, five, six, seven, eight, nine, ten. Any number greater than nine is a combination of two or more numerals.

# PLACE VALUE

| MILLIONS | ONE HUNDRED THOUSANDS | TEN THOUSANDS | THOUSANDS | HUNDREDS | TENS | ONES | |
|---|---|---|---|---|---|---|---|
| 1 | 0 | 0 | 0 | 0 | 0 | 0 | ONE MILLION |
| | 1 | 0 | 0 | 0 | 0 | 0 | ONE HUNDRED THOUSAND |
| | | 1 | 0 | 0 | 0 | 0 | TEN THOUSAND |
| | | | 1 | 0 | 0 | 0 | ONE THOUSAND |
| | | | | 1 | 0 | 0 | ONE HUNDRED |
| | | | | | 1 | 0 | TEN |
| | | | | | | 1 | ONE |

To count to one million,
it is important to understand
PLACE VALUE. Look at the number ten.
It has a one in the tens column and zero
in the ones column. The place we put a numeral determines its value.

Here are some random numbers that will help you learn place value.

Here is the number 8. It has eight in the ones column. Eight!

Here is the number 21. This number has two in the tens column and one in the ones column. Twenty-one!

Here is the number 543. This number has five in the hundreds column, four in the tens column, and three in the ones column. Five hundred forty-three!

Here is the number 6,709. This number has six in the thousands column, seven in the hundreds column, zero in the tens column, and nine in the ones column. Six thousand seven hundred and nine!

When there is no value for a column, a zero holds the place. A zero has no value.

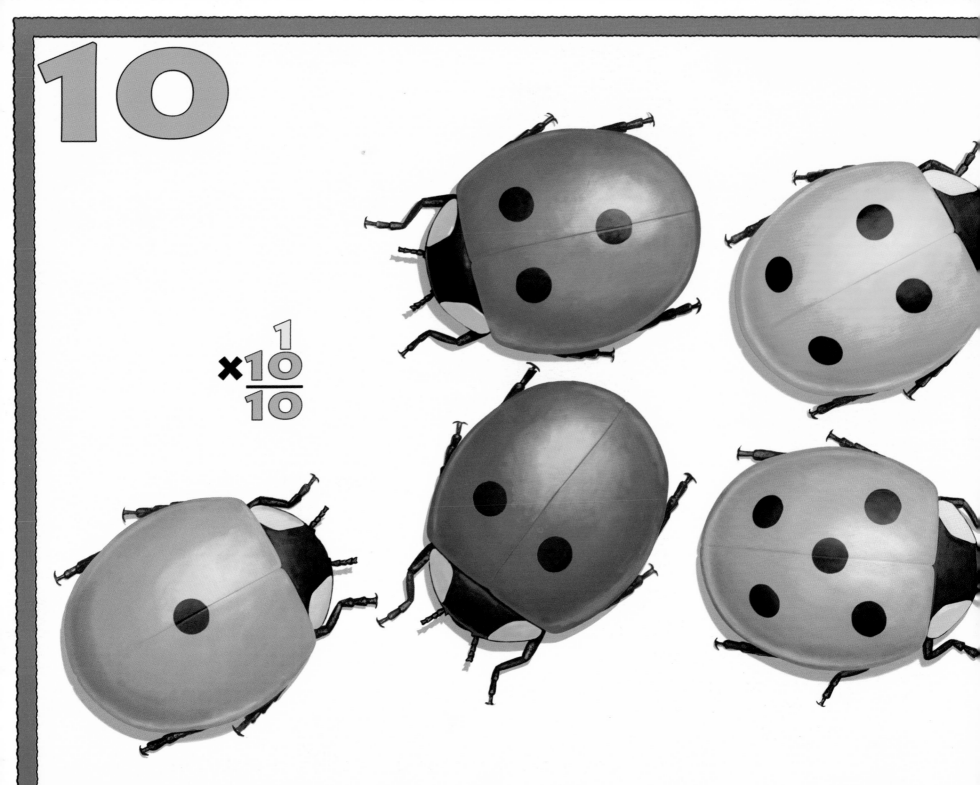

Here are ten ladybugs. One times ten equals ten. This is one group of ten.

You could say you are counting by the power of ten.
Okay, now, on to one hundred.

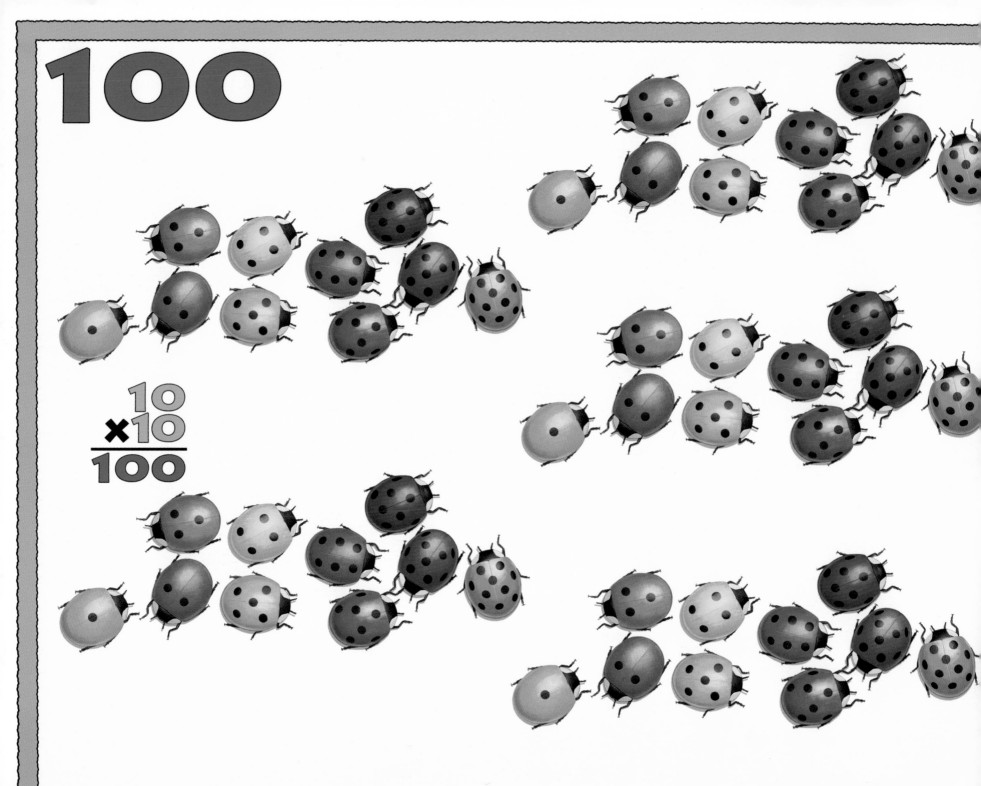

# 100

$$\begin{array}{r} 10 \\ \times\, 10 \\ \hline 100 \end{array}$$

Now there are one hundred pretty ladybugs. Ten times ten equals one hundred.

# ONE HUNDRED

Here is how you counted to one hundred:
ten, twenty, thirty, forty, fifty, sixty, seventy, eighty, ninety,
one hundred. You used the same numerals —1, 2, 3, 4, 5, 6, 7, 8, 9, 0 — but now
they are in the tens column. One hundred is ten groups of ten.

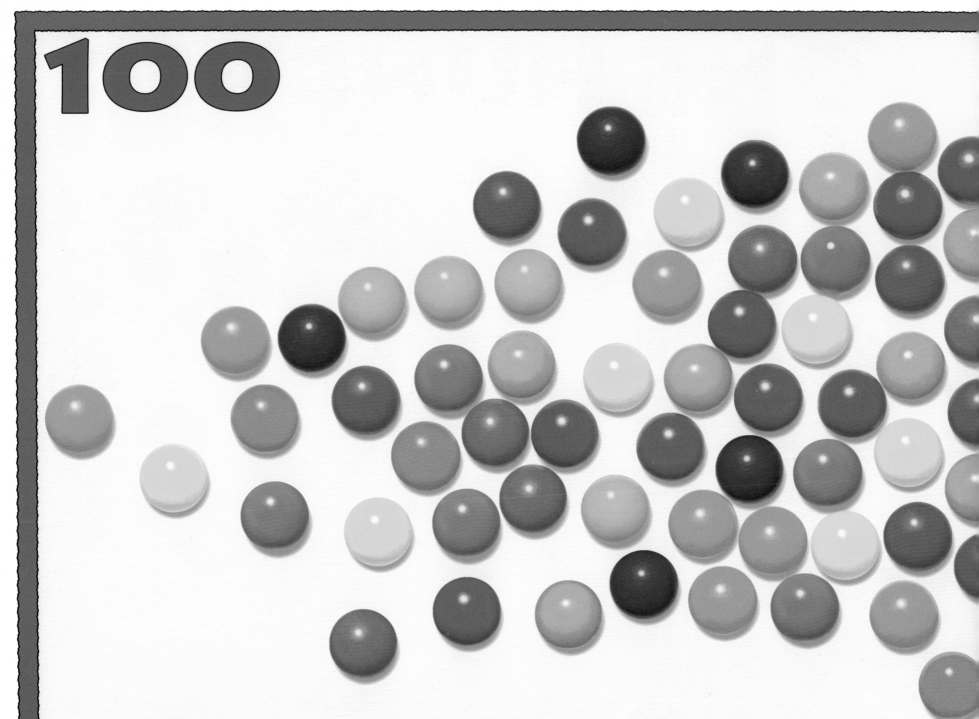

# 100

Here are one hundred gumballs. This is one group of one hundred.
One hundred is a three-digit number. One is in the hundreds column,
zero is in the tens column, and zero is in the ones column.

# ONE HUNDRED

Start chewing. No! Don't touch them. You have to count!
This time, you want to get to one thousand.
Remember the columns—ones, tens, hundreds, thousands.

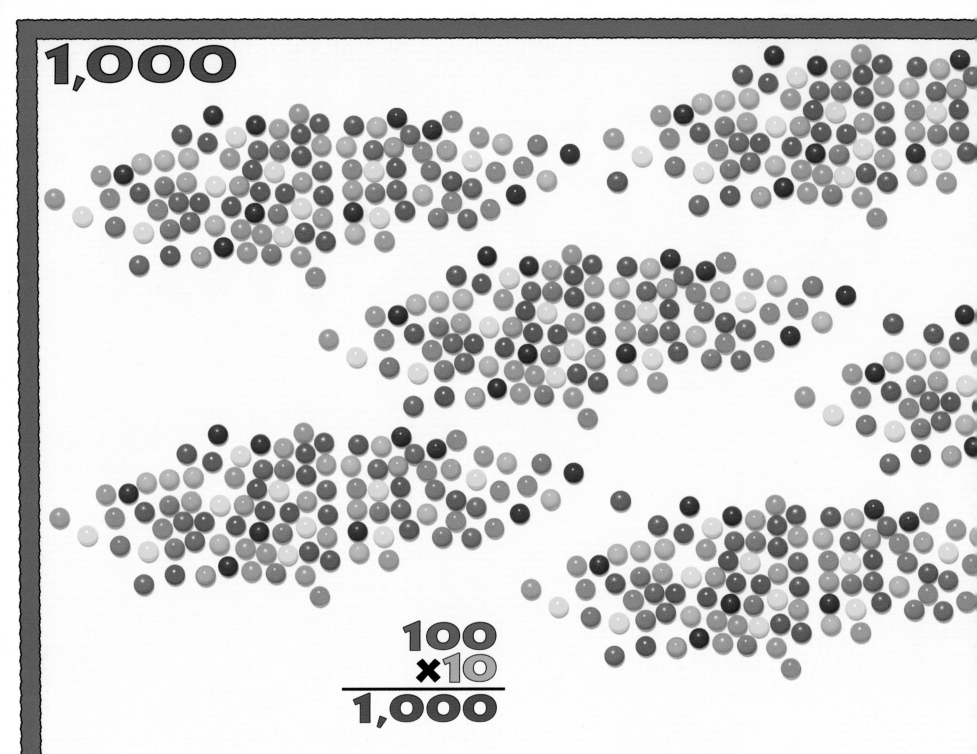

**1,000**

$$
\begin{array}{r}
100 \\
\times\ 10 \\
\hline
1{,}000
\end{array}
$$

Now you have one thousand gumballs.
One hundred times ten equals one thousand. That's a lot of gum!

# ONE THOUSAND

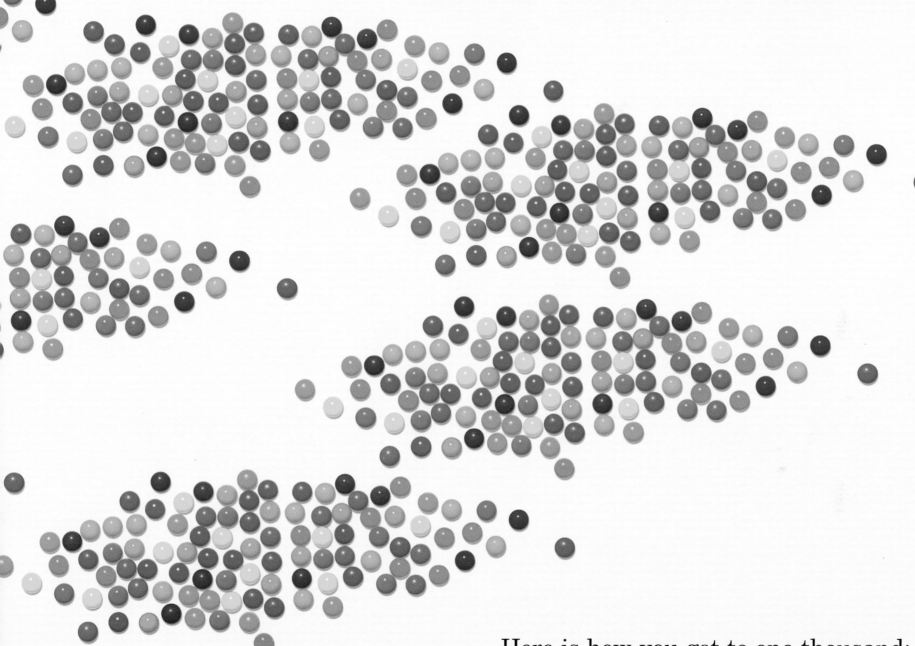

Here is how you get to one thousand:
one hundred, two hundred, three hundred, four hundred, five hundred,
six hundred, seven hundred, eight hundred, nine hundred, one thousand!

# 1,000

The gum attracted ants. Instead of ten groups of one hundred, here is a group of one thousand ants. One thousand is a four-digit number. It has one in the thousands column, zero in the hundreds column, zero in the tens column, and zero in the ones column.

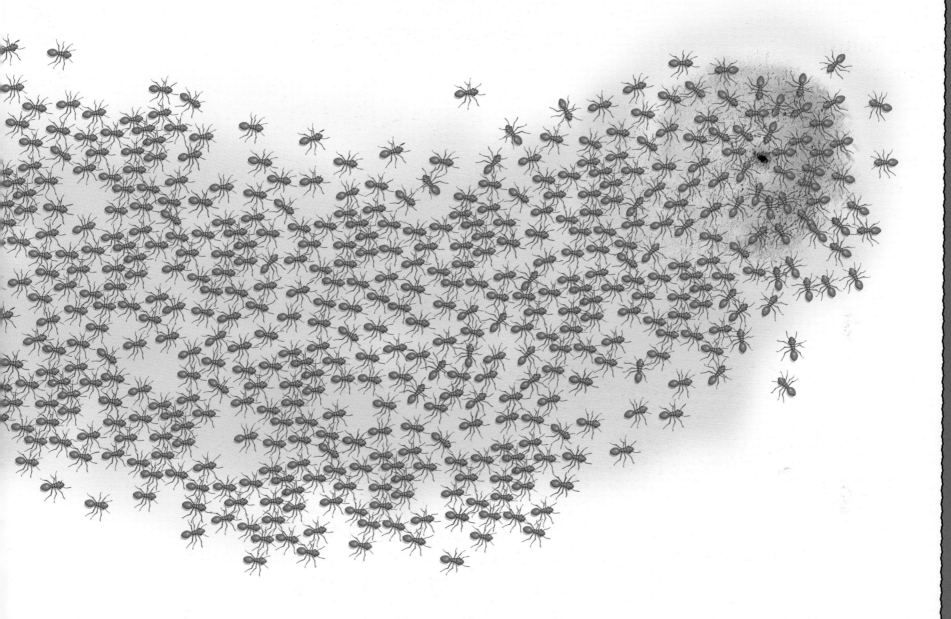

The next column in the place value system is the ten thousands column.
So, let's count to ten thousand.

# 10,000

$$1,000$$
$$\times 10$$
$$\overline{10,000}$$

Count the ten thousand ants before they go underground.
One thousand times ten equals ten thousand.
Ten thousand is a five-digit number.

One thousand, two thousand, three thousand, four thousand, five thousand, six thousand, seven thousand, eight thousand, nine thousand, ten thousand. Ten thousand is one thousand, ten times!

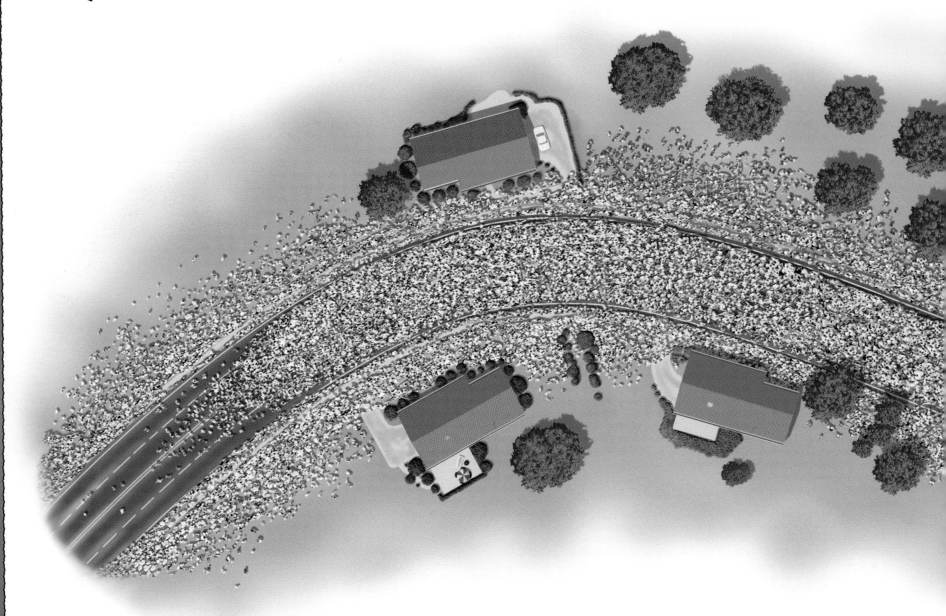

Ten thousand people are running in a marathon.
Each runner is wearing a number from one to ten thousand.
From up high in an airplane, it is hard to read the numbers.

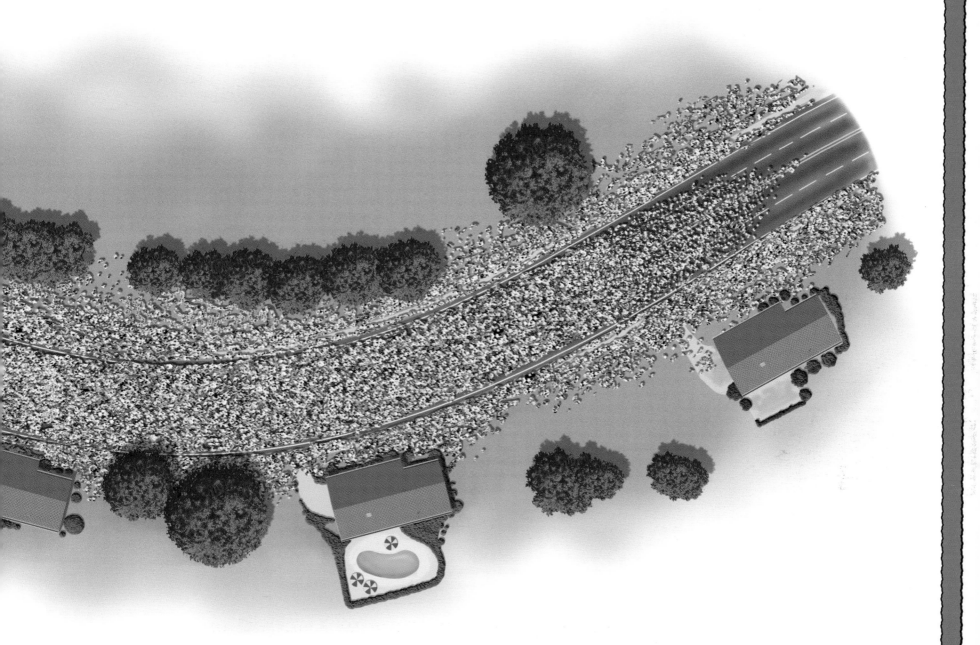

Now you can count in groups of ten thousand up to a six-digit number.

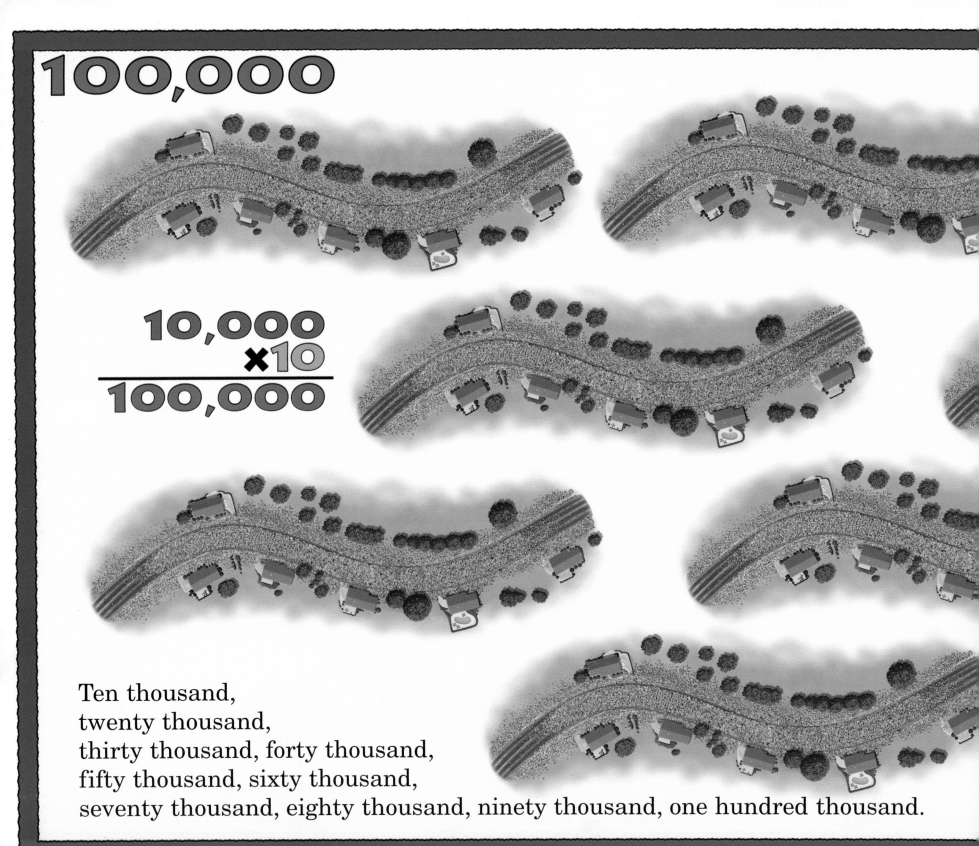

# 100,000

$$10,000$$
$$\times 10$$
$$100,000$$

Ten thousand,
twenty thousand,
thirty thousand, forty thousand,
fifty thousand, sixty thousand,
seventy thousand, eighty thousand, ninety thousand, one hundred thousand.

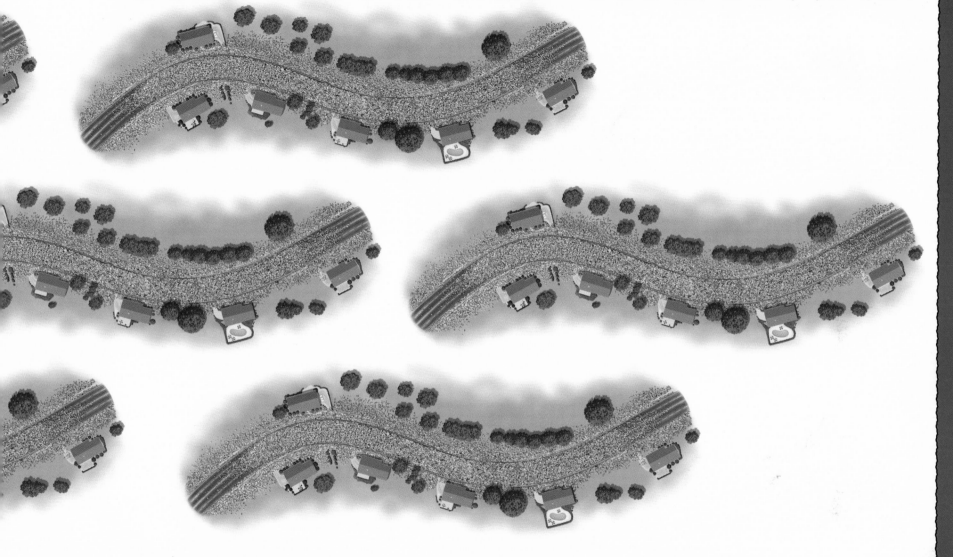

There are now one hundred thousand people running ten marathons.
Ten thousand times ten equals one hundred thousand.
You are getting closer and closer to a million.
You are one tenth of the way there.

# 100,000

This stadium holds
one hundred thousand
screaming sports fans.

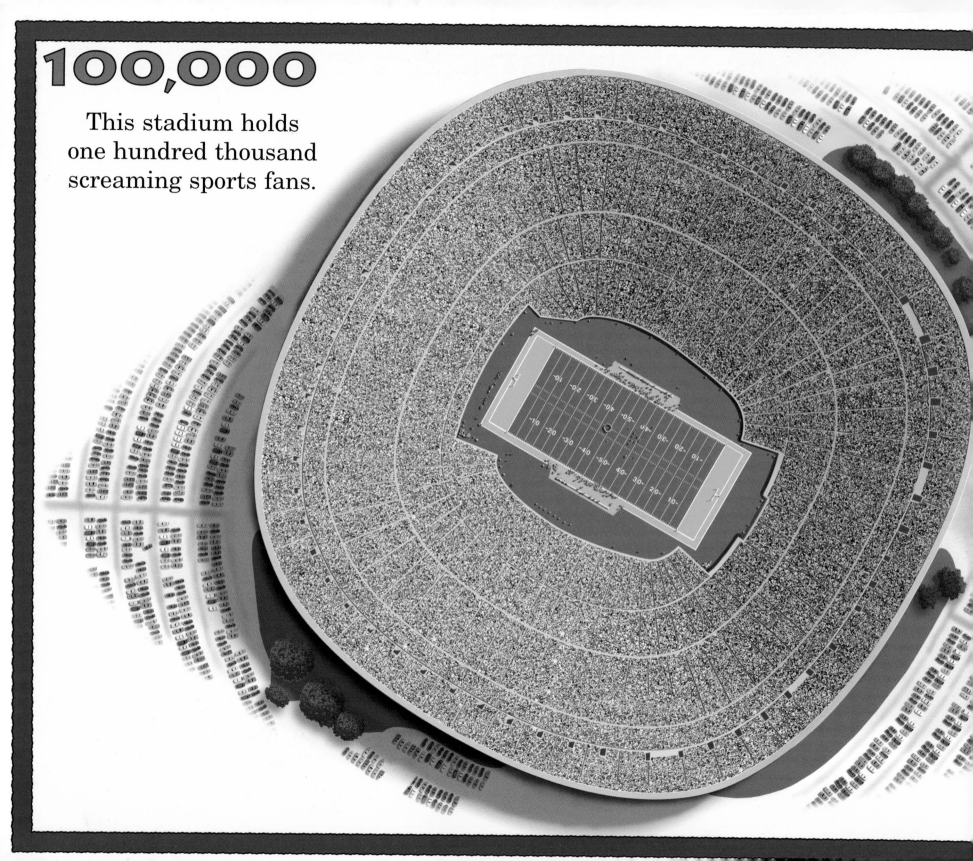

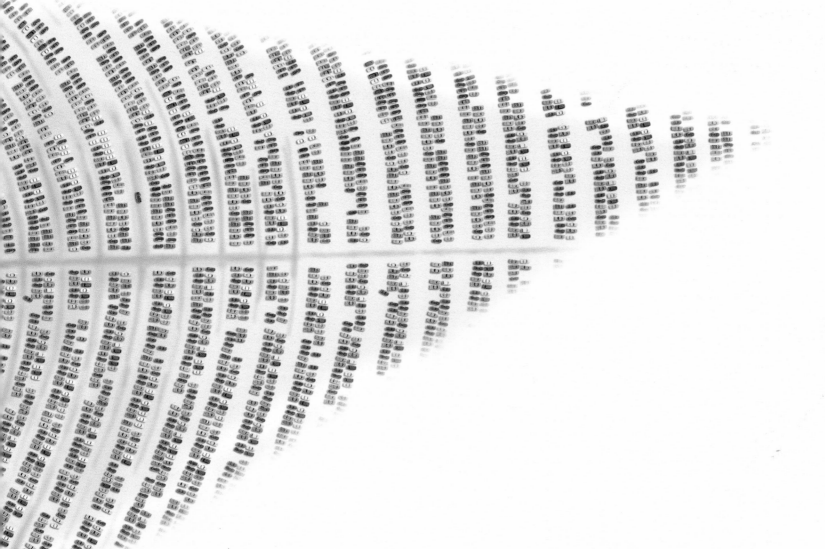

Keep on counting!
Don't count any cars, just count the people.
Using groups of one hundred thousand, use the same
ten numerals to get to one million. 1, 2, 3, 4, 5, 6, 7, 8, 9, 0.

# 1,000,000

One hundred thousand, two hundred thousand, three hundred thousand, four hundred thousand, five hundred thousand, six hundred thousand, seven hundred thousand, eight hundred thousand, nine hundred thousand, ONE MILLION!

$$\begin{array}{r} 100,000 \\ \times\ 10 \\ \hline 1,000,000 \end{array}$$

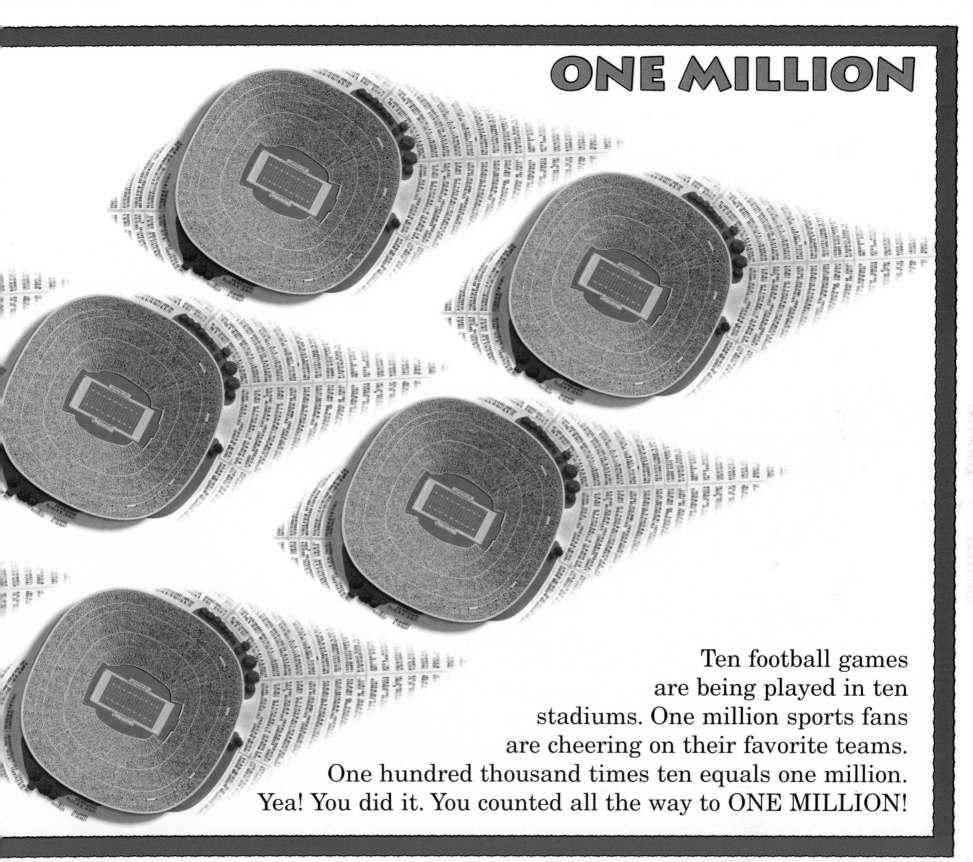

# ONE MILLION

Ten football games
are being played in ten
stadiums. One million sports fans
are cheering on their favorite teams.
One hundred thousand times ten equals one million.
Yea! You did it. You counted all the way to ONE MILLION!

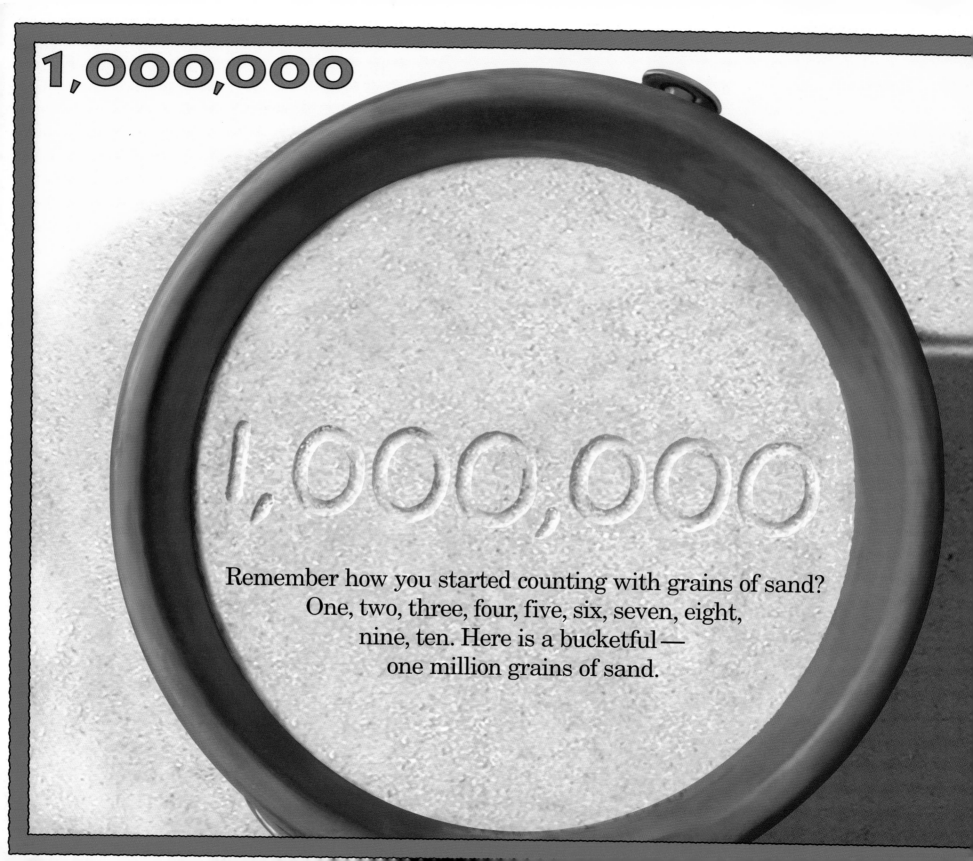

# 1,000,000

Remember how you started counting with grains of sand?
One, two, three, four, five, six, seven, eight,
nine, ten. Here is a bucketful —
one million grains of sand.

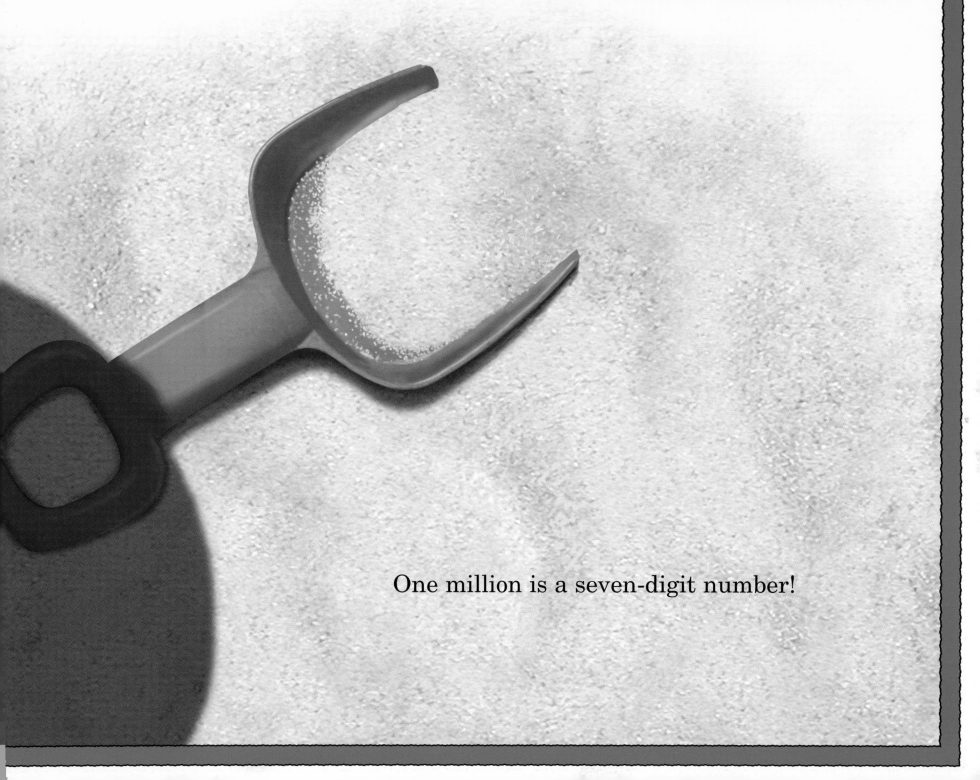

One million is a seven-digit number!

This book started with one earth, the planet we live on.
There is only one earth . . .

. . . but look up in the sky on a clear night. There are millions of stars.
Now you can count to one million, and perhaps beyond. . . .

# ONE MILLION IS:

**1** One, one million times.

**10** Ten, one hundred thousand times.

**100** One hundred, ten thousand times.

**1,000** One thousand, one thousand times.

**10,000** Ten thousand, one hundred times.

**100,000** One hundred thousand, ten times.

**1,000,000** One million, one time!